The Necessity of Wildfire

THE
NECESSITY
OF
WILDFIRE

Caitlin Scarano

BLAIR

Printed in the United States of America
Cover design by Callie Riek
Interior design by April Leidig

*The mission of Blair/Carolina Wren Press is to seek out, nurture,
and promote literary work by new and underrepresented writers.*

We gratefully acknowledge the ongoing support of general
operations by the Durham Arts Council's United Arts Fund
and the North Carolina Arts Council.

Library of Congress Cataloging-in-Publication Data:
Names: Scarano, Caitlin, author.
Title: The necessity of wildfire / by Caitlin Scarano.
Description: Durham, NC: Blair, [2022]
Identifiers: LCCN 2021052190 (print) | LCCN 2021052191
   (ebook) | ISBN 9781949467789 (paperback) |
   ISBN 9781949467796 (ebook)
Subjects: LCGFT: Poetry.
Classification: LCC PS3619.C2678 N43 2022 (print) |
LCC PS3619.C2678 (ebook) | DDC 811/.6—dc23
LC record available at https://lccn.loc.gov/2021052190
LC ebook record available at https://lccn.loc.gov/2021052191

For Calvin

There is no bottom to the night, no end
to our descent.

We suffer each other to have each other a while.
—Li-Young Lee, "Goodnight"

Contents

The Necessity of Wildfire

The houses where they eat the lambs

Wishbone, forked bone
between the neck and breast of a bird

but we are not the bird. Nor the feather, nor
the stone that brought her warm

body down. I am the weak point, a snap,
furcular crack. You are the wish mouthed

against a wall of air. Worm between the ribs.
Smeared blood above a door. Dedication

takes many forms. We stand by these
bleached altars. Gather veins like soft

blue thread in a basket of skin. To not harm
each other is not enough. I want to love you

so much that you have no before. No mother,
no bower, no history of burning doors.

The sea with her rising wet ash. To be marrow
intimate. A crime committed

squatting among the reeds. Add grit
to the skin for texture. Crouch like a toad

beneath the bowl of your skull
and turn the skeleton key in your eye.

Lover, we will know no neighbors. No light
beyond the teeth of a laughing loon.

Every disaster branches out from another

Once, I threw my grandfather's favorite tabby cat
off the back porch. She landed low, trembling
on the bricks my grandmother had laid

in a herringbone pattern a decade before. I can
still remember how slick those mossy bricks were
in the rain, the oak tree choked with ornamental ivy, still

feel my skin snag on the holly bushes where I tried to hide,
still smell the birdbath's fetid water. For years, I thought
what he did to us was simply what was owed

for trying to break the legs of that fucking cat. He caught me
that day, twisted my arm behind my back
and whispered into my ear: *I give you this*

lifetime of fear—a throat full of bees.
He had no idea
the gift I would make of it.

Calf

I am driving by a field. Mountains crusted with a gold decay
surround me. My mother called yesterday; they finally have
a diagnosis. In the field, I notice a cow on her side,
a trembling mass. Sick paternal aunts and cousins
I've never met. I get out of the car and move toward the wire
fence. Inherited autosomal recessive mutation. Watch fluids
rush from her body, matter I cannot name. Slit-lamp
exam of the eyes. Blood draws. Liver function tests.
The black calf beside her. One of my father's
sisters crawling across the living
-room floor. Environmental factors. The mother's low
groans, her obvious distress. All those symptoms finally
under a name, a key turning in my brainstem. But to name
a thing is a trick. The calf a silent creature. Compulsive
seeking. Lesions on my father's face. His twitching
legs. Likely stillborn. I did not attend his funeral. Closer
to dirt than beast. *You probably don't have it,* my mother
says. Despite harmful consequences. I watch the slipping
sun. *Or could just be a carrier.* I return to your car, decide
to do nothing. *Thus, symptomless.* Note how the herd
has already moved on.

During the Wildfires

My body cavernquiet as he kisses my hip. *This taste.*
Salt of a childhood still on me.

I remember sitting on the bench seat of my father's pickup.
The world always passing by through cracked glass. Watching

my mother's father slit the throat of a deer. Wildfire
runs from sternum to cervix. My skin stills

beneath my lover. Rain starts to fall in the skull.
The socket-dry earth screams for it. Who did you last

cross a body of water with? Whose name do you say
even with a throatful of dirt? Until he came, tenderness

hid in me like a cat that went beneath a shed to die.
Save bruises in jars. We are what we collect.

Inside his mouth I find a love letter his mother wrote
to his father years ago. I unfold the letter and find a series

of her sobs no one ever heard. What can I offer you
but this dream of a burning house? Even now my crow

eats his mantle of wasps at the window. Even now,
we hang maps like tapestries. We are where we'll never be

again. Love: the beetle I bit in half. It took me so long to realize
there are people who start fires, not to tend them,

but to see how things burn, and it took me even longer
to realize some places need fire simply to survive.

Song Dogs

When I was eleven, my mother wrote a letter
to her father requesting he stop
molesting her daughters. You should not
drill deeper than two inches
when tapping sugar maples, for fear
of reaching the heartwood. How
such a small distinction
can do so much damage. Anyway, the letter
worked. He became a skin-eating
ghost of his own house. Died grasping
for his aortic root
like the unspared rod. Spring
goes on and on here. Rain falls. Buds
swell. Robins flood the yard. The river
has no time for laughter. Fog tangles
in the tops of the mountain's ciders
like an unwanted crown. These small
hurts. Like the time I closed my fingers
in the truck door and could only say
her name. Blame
between women is tricky like that—promises
sturdy architecture, but only gives you
a paper floor. Two nights in the past month
I've heard a pack of yipping coyotes
surround the house before their own voices

spurred them on. I've drowned and dredged
up so many chapters of myself
just for the sake of the retelling. It's a joke,
though. I've never been on either end
of a snake whip. Never had to save
the thing that devoured
what I loved. Never had to beg the way
the women before me had to beg.

Nights like these I think of my sisters

Girls who live
like flashes in me—crimson,
rage, and eyeteeth. Metal coils
ready to spring.

Photographic flash of the snapshots
my father took of us
on the first day of school
before his leaving. Dazed
by the light in his wake.

Girl, be the flame
who leaps the highest. The one who catches the heavy
velvet curtains on fire and brings down the house.

Never know a mild winter. Never be bell
jar bent. Don't be the rosewood
they take for carving. Don't swoon, don't
apologize, don't polish.

We are the animals between us, not the men,
not the little deaths.

Don't be the silence in the cellar,
the secret buried behind the white barn.

All those years we spent in the forest,
all those latchkey days—don't let

that pinprick hole in your chest
grow to swallow you.

Don't be the horse licking sugar
from anyone's hand. Be the mare that
bolts.

No, be the land beyond the gate
that compels her.

Partition

On my walk this morning, I find a rabbit
in two pieces. First, the loose body, devoid

of spine and legs, and then the head,
perfectly intact, resting two

inches away from the torso. Blood-bright
darling, what did you see? The space between

what happened and what is we imagine. In a dream,
you and I are driving a dirt road through a wildfire.

We are trying to survive each other, we're trying
to get home. When was the last time you spoke

my name? Was it into a cavern so the echo
rebounded, greater than the sum of its parts? Or

did you whisper into a baby shoe and toss it
into the river? Uproot the memory of my tongue

against your tongue. At war with wanting to be
spoken for. The rabbit's eyes are open. The killer

doesn't matter. Grief blood-bright, unspooling, greater
than the sum of its parts. I dreamt the fire

because it was true. Last night, I almost called you
but we're both tired of love

as partition and I cannot make sense of the body
before me, how it was moving one moment,

wrenched and inert the next. How
you were here

for a thousand and sixty-five nights and now
my hands are empty, the rabbit is dead.

In the dream, the fire surrounds us but you
are laughing, certain the rain

is just about to fall.

Unvigil

No to the wood-warping grief. No to this hollow
gown of a bedroom. In a dream, my father says to me,

I have eight months to live. Then he's the size of a jewel
beetle and dies in my hands. This happens

over and over. When I wake up, the bed is almost always
on the ceiling. I cling to it. Not kept by gravity

but the idea of gravity, the way a cat opens her mouth
and makes no sound. I can go

north now or nowhere at all. Learn the names of roving
-eyed constellations. Mistake their stillness

for turning. Mistake our turning for stillness. Lover,
don't you remember? We had a few sons,

but I buried them in snow before their gills disappeared.
You were too busy flooding our house with water

that tasted of bruise. When your shame became uninteresting
to me, I left. No to vigils. No to the endless, sucking hole

of human need. I don't want a beacon,
won't be a beacon. You open a window to let in some air

and a few years fly out like birds or smoke or sheets of paper.
Just like that, they're gone. Your hardwood floor

left soaked in daylight.

In which I dream I am my grandfather

Your girlbody goes under a clawhammer
            cold river. When you come up
you're in *my* skin—the man who made

the man who made you. Every muscle
            pulsing, tensed, every decade
between us wet-mouthed, parted,

reverent. Daughter of my son, my cross,
            my tangled whip, listen: living is actually effortless
if you let the land flood and rot, flood

and rot. If you just let violence rise
            to the surface like cream. Sometimes I crave
the lemon cake she fed me at my first

wedding. I still see the mason jar lights
            strung up in a barn of white
pine blurring behind whiskey shots

and the long shadows of her family's
            minister. I still see the boy in me (the holes
in him) hiding behind hay bales

from a vicious future—the first wife I left
        reeking of copper in a sanitorium, the hammer
I used to try to see the secrets

in my second wife's wasp-paper skull, the war
        of broken ankles I went to but never
spoke of. The way my skin peeled from the steamheat

of Italian restaurant kitchens. The little girls I watched
        playing in the mud on the pond's shore,
their lithe, summer bodies, their sticky

swimsuits. What could I be
        but who I was made to be? The spiked shell
of the snapping turtle you found

on the side of that Virginia road
        picked clean by turkey vultures
long before you could love it.

Not the ending (that came much later) but when we knew it was over

It must have been the time the yard flooded
and all the baby shoes I'd buried
came floating back up.

For him, it might have been
the rabbit's head he found, still singing, beneath my pillow.

When I got drunk beneath a harvest moon and shot
a pistol into the river, aiming at nothing and everything.

Maybe it was decided before us—the night my father
slept in the cemetery
before finally skipping town, the day he married my mother
in a windowless courtroom, or that bar in Key
West where they met and danced
by the night-still water.

It might have been the midnight sun, the alpenglow wrung
out, that squatter cabin held together by ghosts, or the night
the ice gave up the Susitna while we camped on its banks.

His blood in this snow. How I named him sick until it was true.

Mornings I felt like a nag
or a mother or a monster.

Mornings I felt nothing but the rot of light already in my bones.

Or that he never brought up my father's death after it happened.
That we seemed bored
by each other's greatest moments of need.

Maybe it was simple—when I started sleeping
on the couch, when the house
became a series of divvied rooms and the slamming
of doors, when the thing lost its wonder.

Or the day his little brother got married
and we danced close beneath mason jar lights, laughing,
knowing it would never be us.

On his deathbed, my father, who I haven't seen in ten years, offers me homemade moonshine

Did you think it would come to this? That you'd be begging
the mirror you stuck your fist through
to put itself back together. You can't
stitch glass. You can't call home. You can't love
just one part of a person.

After this, I'll know how things leak, that death
begins in slow drips. Your body will go down
a shower drain one canary-yellow drop at a time.

To make moonshine: 5 gallons of water, 8.5 pounds
of cracked corn, 1.5 pounds of crushed
malted barley, a pinch
of yeast. Foreshots and heads: pray
that you distill past the threat
of blindness. Hearts: ripe as years bloody
and beating on the branches of an apple tree. Take more
than you can consume and the whole bushel rots.
Tails: you'll know when the sweetness runs thin, slick
to the touch. Feints and cuts. Set these jars
aside for an uncertain future.

After this, I'll love and leave five men
in two years. After this, I'll check the underside of my mattress

for mold from the sweat of all their bodies. I'll count
the rocks on the bottom of a dive bar's
bathroom floor. After this, I won't be mad. I'll learn
to save my anger for those willing
to fight back.

They Named You Patriarch

In July 2020, the Washington Department of Fish & Wildlife reported the natural death of wolf 32M, the first wolf to establish a pack in the Central Cascades in 100 years and the former breeding male of the Teanaway pack[1]

The hillsides were on fire
that year you came down. *Timid*
with an unassuming
face. It is late August.
The night delivers
mountains to my lonely
doorstep, murmurs of winter.
Each season disappears
like a snake swallowing
its tail. All I can think about
is how few summers
we each get. The air soft
with years. You had twelve,
long for a wolf.
In the video of researchers
collaring you, I study the pads

1. WDFW press release: "The wolf 'patriarch' of the central Cascades," https://wdfw.wa.gov/species-habitats/at-risk/species-recovery/gray -wolf/updates/wolf-patriarch-central-cascades

of your feet—massive & made
to be worn down. I read
about the progeny you sired,
wolves that dispersed
across the state, some all
the way back to British
Columbia, where you came
from. Or the son who left
Teanaway with you
and later joined the Naneum
pack. How you set off
on your own then, almost
as if you just had to see
him off first. How stillness
finally finds us. The air
was soft, your radio
collar emitting a mortality
signal from the creekbed
where you laid down.

Wellspring

My fingers in your mouth, I find a soft history
of caverns, echoes of the last
two women who loved you—your wife
and the one after. How much flows
underground without us knowing?
When we were in Oregon, we hiked
to the headwaters of the Metolius.
It didn't look like much, water bubbling
from a slit in the embankment. What we see
is deceptive—a slow trickle, 50,000 gallons
per minute. Kokanee salmon, rainbow
trout, bull trout, and mountain
whitefish. All those years I spent toiling
upstream. Wellspring, my god,
how I hunted you. Followed the tracks
of a snowshoe hare through a decade
of drifts. Hindfoot and forefoot. Followed
small drops of blood from my bedroom
to yours, like Gretel and her little stones.
At the headwaters that day, you took
a picture of us, our backs to the mountain. I kept
my eyes open despite the unrelenting light.
To think you were a stranger not so long ago
and now I'm inside of you. Cold,
clear, constant. Tributaries gather.

The fen fills with wildflowers—aster, pearly
everlasting, blazing star. Fish spawn
and rot. Ribbon grass takes over. You will
suffer. I will suffer.

Buttercream

I cut open an avocado only to find it dappled
with rot. I eat it anyway. Because my blood
burns, I decide not to have children. My father's
father was full of copper. His son, a liver
textured with scarring. I ate it anyway.
I asked for guidance, not a leash and a collar.
I turn my belly inside out—it's dappled
with eggs the color of buttercream. My hens
don't know which are fertilized
and which aren't. My mother lost her wedding
ring in vegetable garden dirt. I dig
out the rot. I say I decided
not to have children but no man
ever asked me and meant it. If each parent gives you
a defective gene, you can bake a cake
or crawl across the floor between buckets
of your blood. I dig but never find
the ring. Some hens sit on eggs
until they rot. Some men take hammers
to their wives. My lover yawns.
Of all the stories I could tell, I've learned
of all the stories you could tell. Her blood
burned. My mother made a red
velvet cake with buttercream frosting.

She ate the whole thing. She never told anyone
who believed her. He might have been
sick his whole broken bowl
of a life. I might find a golden ring
around my iris. I might not
be a creature versed in dirt. Anger,
like memory, takes away as much
as it provides. Some hens leave their eggs
where they land. Either way, we
follow. We gather. We eat them.

Leveret at Laughing Jaw

Mother made a nest in the dead
mouth of what almost killed her. She was resourceful

in that way, never wasted a sprig or a stone.
I was young, unsung, curled up

as the young often are. My sisters and I
planted a fringed tulip bulb in his eye

socket, picked clean, and filled it with loam.
By spring, what sprouted had many fingers,

most of them accusing, some of them silent.
At night, my mind laid flat as a clearing and the hours

crept through like timid deer. When the moon
light hit them, their bodies twisted, turned

to half liquid, half smoke and suspended a few feet
above the earth—spiraling, morphing.

One night, one real night, I stood outside
my cabin and watched the aurora evolve and stretch

like taffy being spun, foolish enough then
to think I knew her suffering or the type of woman

I would become—the damage my mouth,
in all its green, would inflict.

Parameters

My mother gave me a diary with two little keys
when I was a child, with my rotten
gods, useless locks, secrets no one wants to hear.
Until you're an adult fucking
a man who wraps your hair around
his right hand like reins, says, *Tell me
what you were like as a little girl.* I'll tell you—
back then I kept this great
scream in my body,
a prescribed burn
that jumped the break. Stomach
in tatters. I wasn't the one killing
animals with chains and sticks. I was
the one watching the boy next door
do the killings. Summers I led my little sister
to this pond so still and foul. We swam
but somehow knew not to touch
bottom. *Tell me what you (were) like.* I memorized
exit, memorized matchbox, made myself
small enough to fit through a cat door.
There were days when we laughed,
days we grew teeth. Season to sow,
season to reap.

Deer Season

This morning, woodstove smoke mixes with fall fog. I watch the river for signs of how it will flood as it leaves these mountains for the Salish Sea. I live in northwest Washington now but grew up in southeastern Virginia, the Piedmont Region. I remember Virginia summer most vividly, moving through humidity like wading through brackish water. There were so many bugs back then—fleas, lice, deer ticks. Horseflies biting as my sisters and I swam in the reservoir. Our father watched from the shore, sipping whiskey and singing James Taylor songs to no one, certainly not us.

I read recently that the core of repulsion is recognition.

My partner asks what Virginia was like. I want to tell him it's a song I hate but can't stop singing. In the summers, men and machines macerated the field between our startled house and the railroad tracks, raked the grass into tight bales the shape of marshmallows. In September, my sisters and I climbed the bales, pulled ourselves up by the golden twine like mountaineers. We watched the sun sink, an egg yolk behind the trees.

In this field, we were stalked by the women we'd become, shadowless foxes. One carried a box cutter and a fistful of red doll hair. Another carried a daughter. The last had nothing but an empty mother-blue pitcher. Like archaic clockwork, Norfolk

Southern cars carried coal from the Blue Ridge to the sea. Ethos of industry, towns that ripen and then rot in the wake.

I used to believe time was a line.

On the first day of deer season, the boys were allowed to miss school, while the rest of us sat in those desks as if strapped in. Each July, the local fathers reenacted Lee's Retreat in that field. Our mother watched my sisters and me watch the men rehearse. We yawned, slapped at flies, already unmoved by the pageantries of masculinity. Such war games. *If you're shot, you have to stay down*, I heard one of them yell. *Those are the fucking rules.*

I still have a shoebox of horseflies, a history of hammers snapped at the neck, secrets whispered through a screen door. It was summer once—we were children. Waist-deep in the places we weren't allowed. At church, I was told to sit very still, like a baby rabbit in clover. Behind the twisted magnolia, my best friend's cousin made her undress for him. I imagine she can still smell the rotting eggshell-white petals. The summer we turned sixteen, we swam a mile across Lake Gaston and nearly drowned. That night we returned to the water, swam naked under a full moon.

We were all children once. Virginia splitting apart each thread of my hair while I gnawed on a corncob, listening for a lull in the fighting of blue jays.

There are things I'm trying not to mention—the time I held myself under at the Fort Pickett pool until the world was all popped balloons of color. The shape of a two-month-old after she was shaken to death. The kicked-in back door, the doors I couldn't lock in time. The men we knew best, what they did to us behind panes of silence. Or the mapped heart chambers of the twelve-point whitetail our neighbor killed from the deer stand I mistook for a treehouse. Separate from the tree where he hung them by their feet to drain the blood.

What was it like? Dense, it was so dense back then. A world of white-and-black dairy cows knee-deep in grass, tobacco fields for miles, kudzu smothering a hillside, and abandoned silos like watchtowers. It is a place that seems to give so much—fertile countryside dense with this country's history and generations of old families like taproots. But really, it takes more than it provides. A bucolic landscape that hides households brimming with desperation, prejudice, and violence.

The tall grass where we walked between waiting copperheads. The menagerie of beasts who taught me what I am.

There were horses a half-mile away. My sisters and I used to take them bitter apples from the trees we inherited. They were always very careful with their teeth, and we were careful to push our palms skyward.

Fast Beauty

Follow a line of ants
back to her bedroom, cage
of barbed afternoon light.
Days I couldn't leave
but wanted to, nights
I didn't stay but meant
to. Fears like wooden toy
horses. The hand mimics
galloping. Somewhere
an invitation slides
under a door, I push
the top of my body
through a window, the tongue
sparks like a flint, a girl
doesn't love
a boy. I wanted some of her
war, not this litany
of sobs she saved that
no one ever heard.
The first time I said *I love you*
I was asleep. She was
listening. She remembers
me in the coldest seasons.
Remembers kissing sloppy
in our early twenties

on a snowy street corner,
the time I cut my own
hair with rusted
scissors. Remembers
how I called her father
cruel. She was afraid of fire.
I was afraid of faking it. Now
I'm doorstep-savvy, sober,
morning-eyed and hemmed
in habits. Growing a life from
regret-rich soil. She gets married
in a strapless dress, her bride
wears a crown of gold leaves.
Thank god, I think. But for what—
her happiness? How I failed?
I've never met anyone who
seemed to care for me
like she did. I listen
to music we listened
to back then, trap a Midwestern
town in a snow globe. I shake it
and shake it for the fast beauty
but don't know what to do
next besides simply set it down.
The man I live with now
teaches me to use an axe.
His instructions are simple—

center your body where
you mean to aim. Follow
the weight where it leads.
In one motion, make a clean,
unwavering split.

**I know we're all sick of poems with deer
but let me explain**

Last night: a forest of hospital beds

I want to ask all these strangers: do you ever think
every day you're getting closer to your death or do you wake
in the morning with hope crusted in the corners
of your eyes, your teeth
already grinning at the air?

Grief is a very complex machine, it told me so itself, a matrix
that takes years

                 A. to navigate
                 B. from you like teeth

Dear J, I have a few acres all to myself now, you should see them

I'm sorry you had to turn so many stones
while I looked on at a careful distance

The male human heart at age 36
        Who knew, I guess, what can give
        out

It's true that I didn't mind the horses starving outside
my window, as long as they came when called

I had many apples going to rot,
            what else could I have done

I read about how the water in Lake Superior
            is replaced
            every 191 years

Remember the spot where I dove under
and was rolled by a wave and for a moment
I did not know what was up or down, what was past
            or present, you or him—

That winter, the lake froze, trace lines of cracks
in the ice colliding, the fractures in my body all met

In another dream, you're in front of me—solid, tangible,
with a dark beard and corduroy pants
I ask you about dying and you say, *Let's go to this city I know*
Then you disappear into a tangled forest
and I follow, stumbling, ripped by thorns

You're always just out of reach, always
just turning the next corner

Remember those children we watched while we ate ice cream
on that green bench in Sault Saint Marie?
            That isn't my favorite memory of you, not by far,
            but it's the one I keep
            coming back to

I took it so I should have wanted it
But the sugar made my teeth ache

Every memory is two-sided, like that day we lay in the grass
watching ships pass through the lochs
        Distance is deceptive
        It was sunny, the photos you took prove it
        But the wind—

Or the wind and the rain that day we met
at the lighthouse, you wore a black sweater, I hadn't seen you
        in years, you looked younger, time
        doing its mirror trick

The scene draws us
We weren't ghosts but we were
both adrift, though only one of us knew it

When I reach the city you spoke of,
it's been abandoned for decades

Every memory is two-sided, like the time you were driving
and your Jeep hit
        black ice and spun out
Like the time I was driving and my car died
as we coasted downhill
        All this foreshadowing for nothing

In a human dream, electric blue hydrozoan
creatures blossom in the Superior's deepest water

Every memory is two-sided, and your story isn't mine to claim

I run these dirt trails near my house, I think of you,
I touch my chest, count my breaths
        so my heart keeps going

One day I came upon this mother deer and two
fawns, they were tiny, spotted, legs so ready to give
out but they did not give out

Josh, you should have seen them.

Lady of the Shovel

For Megan

It is the year she imagines leaving, her trail
through snow like a graphite line across paper. Land

of the steady hand. Land where we only kill in the name
of need. To finally see the trees

for the forest, to leave nothing but a room
quivering inside a house—imagine. The raven

who hangs around both streetlights & stars teaches her
how to spell *feast* without *fist*. She doesn't

yet know that her sisters will search all night, mouthing
her delicate name into every discarded

exoskeleton. Not once will the dead ever
wake. Still, we'll save a side of the cup just for her

to drink from. Years of milk, years of squalor. Palaces
we'll make of spruce boughs and tattered blue

tarp. Men will come and go like children. Children
will come and go like sandhill cranes.

She'll be royalty somewhere—waited on, carefully pried apart, revered. Every scar cataloged.

As she leaves, she swears she hears the raven's last laugh like a rusty gate.

Some thoughts on the one who said I expected too much

My mistake to try to architect astonishment from everything,
even the snakeskin we found in the attic
the day of your cousin's wedding. She was ankle-length
and sternum bones. I could count them. We only
danced to one song. You were wrong about Virginia. Wrong
about the color of my eyes. Wrong to judge me
ungentle. Must have been all that static
snow in your ears or the fear you wrought into a father's
hatchet. I was the line finally gone taut, winter
of want, the pike sucked from water, beating my spine
against the ice. Four years you accused me
of a barking dog. Four years I dreamt a flock of floating
baby shoes. I laughed at a crown
of firethorn and poison ivy.
Laughed while my forehead bled, laughed
like this was what we wanted. I lied to you
about so much, but the mercy, the mercy
I mouthed for was true. Now a lover asks what I want—
to have my hair pulled? To reign? To be blue
smoke? All of it, all of it. He plants nut trees, talks
in terms of palimpsest instead
of damage, saw a cedar shake house by a green river
and built it, can you imagine? You could barely get out
of the truck to help me. You could barely

hold my voice in cupped palms. Couldn't
believe I kicked in a door when a door needed
to be kicked in. A body can be made
brave, husk back bracts to the meat,
to the throat-red ruby, to the clearest voice in me, both
childless and unchildlike. I forgive myself
my hunger because it propelled me to cross
that lithium-streaked lake between us.
As long as it doesn't bite or linger, your ghost may pass
through here. You may even eat of my table, I am that
steeltoed now, flexible of bone,
christened of dogtooth.

Not how the silo stood but what it was after the fire

It's just before daybreak. You're running. You can hear men crowing. No—roosters crowing in the rotting barn that will burn down in less than a year. Or is it a decade? The cement silo ring will be the only thing left standing. In this one, the fly is trapped between the storm window and the outer glass. You are a child. I mean—your mother is a child, dressed in a nightgown. She's crowing, by which I mean crying. Or laughing. Who can really tell? Your grandparents are meeting for the first time. Your grandmother, a child, offers him a fly. I mean a stick of gum. *I will have the marriage I imagined.* He locks a girl in a bathroom with a clawfoot tub. The fly is caught between your skin and fat. Between your tongue and your teeth. She's running. She's dressed in white or rust or blame. You turn a corner in the alley and a man materializes. I mean really—it feels like he was hiding between the panes of air. He says, *Don't run. They always run.* You're running through. You're lying. *You better kill me before I kill you.* You made it up. Her dress is muddied. Her hands are muddied. Your eyes are clear. Your teeth are crowded and ready and even though you don't say much now, later you will be the woman who won't stop speaking and laughing and nagging and fucking. I have a box of hands and dolls' heads. He steps closer. Your little sister raises the cast-iron skillet in defense. No, she raises only daughters. She's crying. He's crying. His head between his hands, he says to me, *I can't keep up.* She's a mother, a daughter, a sister. Your niece. They always run. She's dragging a doll by its wrist. It is your doll or your grandmother's doll or your grandmother. The head of it knocks against the baseboard and you're reminded of the cow pasture. The night he kicked in the back door. The night she woke with your scream in her mouth and reached for a baseball bat. The night her father drove her, you, no, the daughter who wasn't born, to the abortion clinic in Brooklyn because it was illegal where you lived then. You're in the cow pasture, barefoot in the snow, where he threw all of your belongings. Years later, he laughs at you, *Gender isn't a fucking construct.* And spits into a bucket. It runs, you run. My mother was seventeen. I am seventeen when he says, *I will knock your teeth from your head.* Like snow, they'll fall. My old sister's belongings tossed into a winter pasture. A knock on the door in the night. You know the sound of a doll head, a woman's head, against his curled hands, against a floorboard, against a hammer. Stop it. This isn't the story you're supposed to tell, or it isn't your story to tell, or you've told it enough. Which is it, then? *Enough.* Not enough. There is a fly between these words. A fly caught in my eye socket. I can't seem to run fast enough. My teeth, my mouth, are so muddied. All this fucking, by which I mean confessing. I have a box of his spit. There is a pasture and a cement ring that was left after a fire and I can't think of a better way to tell you this. I have a box of her hair. She's not dressed in white. She is not a gown or a bride or a doll. She's not anything. He came out of the air. He reached for me. He took to her skull. He drove her in the night. He flung the hatchet. He was just a boy. There are stories without monsters, stories without morals. How do you know if I'm lying? How will you know if it is a laugh or a howl that escapes her mouth after she feasts on survival like a wolf over the bowels of the stomach that opened readily beneath this hunger? I have a box of flies. Some are dead, but some are quite alive.

A Poem to Multiple Men

Who made and mended my wrists
of wire. Copper conductors of heat
and electricity. Think of the synaptic
dance, jaw loose daze as you bend
me over and peer inside. I keep you
around to witness the holes in me
I can never see. In the morning we part
wordless, mired mouths, semen on my chest,
the sun rapping against my window
like a chipper neighbor in need of sugar.
I learned the price of loving
a place more than a person: that's how
I lost one. Were we ever happy? I wrote
and then stomped through each creek bed
between our bodies with knee-high
galoshes. Most days I take a girl
for a mask. I hide my teeth behind
my hair and pretend to love snow. Give me
the boy with the belly of an ox, give me
one like a child's tower of blocks
that I can knock down and rebuild
until the game tires of us. I hope you find
someone who loves you. I was never the girl
next door, I was the one cackling beneath

the radiator, bruising herself behind
the eyes. Chasing the moonsure,
the white dog, the man who left me
with a tongue of coal dust.
He's really no different than the boy
I made into jigsaw and kissed in the rain
until one of us bled.

God's Country

Summer here is pastoral. Verdant valleys against gunmetal mountains. *Entrance to the American Alps.* The sign on the edge of town creaks on its hinge in front of abandoned houses. My paranoia ebbs and flows. The hillsides—scraped of their trees and topsoil by human industry—wait to give out. A cluster of squatters live near the trail I jog—white men with tangled beards, dressed in open coats too thick for this hot weather. They watch with precision as I pass. Does violence sleep? While we dream, the river erodes the earth beneath the two-lane highway that snakes from here to the Salish Sea. Last January, three miles away, a man chained a woman to the toilet in his motor home and tortured her, shot heroin into her ankle. *This is God's country,* my mother says when she visits. I drive her up Washington Pass where snow still shines back at the sun in linen white patches. *Human remains found of man missing since 2014,* I read in the local paper. His friend, suspected of murder but never charged, died in 2015, though there are no details or obituary online. Our garden pushes up more kale and collards than we can eat. Rumor spreads of one of the local restaurant owners trafficking women through Canada. His restaurant business thrives as the town bloats with tourists. The hens we raised chatter just outside the screen door. In a gorge, a park ranger finds the body of a man who went missing near Thunder Creek a month ago hanging from a tree. Outside our window, a barred owl's cry pries open the night like a tin can. My partner mistakes the sound for a human infant, but I swear I hear a woman screaming. In morning light, he tends the land he just bought—turns soil, rips out root wads, claws down rotten planks of scabbed fencing, fights back invasive blackberry patches with a machete—comes out covered in nicks and nettle stings. I read that when the woman finally escaped, still handcuffed, she fell to her knees in front of a passing car. *This place*, he says, grinning, *I think we can heal it.*

Spur

The night your father left for good
he slept in a cemetery then set out
at first light. You were five.

> Your god did not come.
> No beast

with a halo of antlers
to carry you on.
That obsidian stone you coughed up
and kept beneath your pillow

> never staved off any loss.
> Every talisman failed you.

The family collie wore a half-moon
into the cracked dirt

trying to get at the rooster when
he tore open your sister's back
along the spine with his spur.

> But she never reached him.
> She couldn't save anything

from her chain. Your mother
must have paused by the kitchen
sink one morning and sobbed
into a dish towel until
she could hardly breathe.

                Then she collected herself

and raised three daughters,
while her husband razed his body
like a barn that had outlived
its use. She taught you

how to leave a man
when he decides to shape himself
into a cinder block and asks you
to hold the rope.

Your grandfather killed a deer, my grandfather killed a deer

You tell me you have good memories of stringing up
a deer with your grandfather.
You were fifteen. You were careful
at skinning it, careful at gutting it. Your little brother
cut too deep, poked a hole in the stomach.
You listened to the gas
escape. You know about the men
we each come from, pronged, bloodshot
legacies, how we learned who to be
and who not to be. My grandfather was a hunter
too, but a different breed. Helped his wife kill her
first buck. Tried to lock his second daughter away,
trapped his granddaughters in a bathroom
with a clawfoot tub. Violence I locked shut
like an ammunition box when I left home
at seventeen. *You gut it in the field*, you say,
not the shop. A place for every act.
Could I have known you before all this? Familiar,
your voice. Your mouth on my wrist.
Familiar, my body curled against
yours. Mollusk shell, keeping
the soft parts in. You never asked
too much of me. On one of our last
walks together, it is night. You pass under

lamplight like water, a few feet out of reach. There,
beside the sidewalk, a doe and her yearling.
So close, I can see the clouds of their breath
hanging in the air. Back then, you hung the meat
in strips to cure. Your family ate it and you ate it,
became strong, became the man I know now
fifteen years later, careful at being gentle,
careful. You remember the shot
at a decent buck, the shot you didn't take
because you'd lost sight of them,
your brother and grandfather. What we decide
not to do. The families we have,
the ones we'll choose. Sons I saw when you showed
me pictures of you as a boy. Your face, my face,
how it all ran together. The person you'll love
after me, like an animal you've always been
closing in on and I will be alone in a clearing, putting
my body back together, unstripped, ungutted,
unskinned. The urban deer we find do not startle.
They just walk away. *The feet and trimmings we fed
to Grandpa's German shepherd*, you said.
The one he taught you not to turn
your back on. *How he loved
the bones.*

Oxbow

What good is a long life? The river smells
of where it comes from

not where it is going. I've never lived
by water until this. I grew up between dairy

fields and oak-pine forests. Sisters
hiding behind a crushed

velvet window curtain. Girl,
static, ghost. There was a clock

high on the wall in the living
room. One night, I swear, the sound

grew so loud. My blood's ticked ever
since. Travel far from where they raised you

and your blood will still burn.
In a dream, the lower half of my body

is buried in snow. The rest scatters
for sky. Along the river, a conspiracy

of crows take up in a white pine. A bevy
of swans follow. The contrast is too much

for the field to contain. Someone asked me
my greatest subject. *Shame*, I said

without thinking. My lover keeps a folding
knife in the bottom drawer of his dresser.

I like to take it
out when he isn't here. Dig little

notches into the back of our headboard
with the tip. One for every secret

we or the water withhold.

Diobsud Creek Pack

April 2019

after winter
descend mountains
a worm moon in
everyone
through everyone
the bluest grief
men
when solitary
radio
news of home
crush
between
stained fingers
by water
in a dream
of salt
crashing
rumored bodies
wildernesses
neck snare unseen
in a deer
in a flooded field
howling
the spine
opening

you'll see fire
catch the glint of
your lover's eye
will pass
hunger
will win out
will follow you
collar you
coordinates
radius of wander
the bud
incisors
anger apertured
to foam
that tastes
of fortitude
over boulders
invented
haven or
your death
hollow
I'll hear you
lighting up
whole mountainsides
at the seams

Daughter Knot

Detached from context, deer spine you find
engulfed in bodilessness. That night, a sky veined

with unresolved stars. They throb and a future
sickness nags at you, a honey locust

thorn in your side. Ulcers blossom in your intestine, needy
purple mouths. Abuse begets abuse, the unwell

beget the unwell. Grief like ribbons in a girl's hair, her teeth
catching the sun. You bend over your father's grave

as if it's a mixing bowl, as if he is a task you have
to complete. Another day of rain opens like a sinkhole.

You cut off your hair. It hisses when you toss it
into the wood stove; your lover watches

from a chosen distance. How much can his blood
dilute? You dream in organs. Egg lump on the breast,

copper in the brain, knot in your throat. All this talk
of children, you'd rather speak of snakes. You'd

rather spit it out and offend than choke
on the offer.

Ember

He says when we're fucking he can almost feel us
becoming one person. I forgot what it meant

to love this way—teeth against the back of thigh, his
voice like a snake around my spine, to see his death

every time he leaves the house—I forgot so much.
Last night, I could not stop eating his hair. I held it

like cake between my fingers, and wasn't a self
nourished in the dreaming? Healing, like everything

else, was not what we expected. But I knew
to follow a river, to turn away

from every baby-filled basket in the rushes, every
lover promising me their best rib. There is no good

or evil here. But touch me gently. If there is a god,
I'd have found him by now squatting beneath

a stone like an unblinking toad. Though I believe
in ghosts. I've seen them holding their splayed

throats up to my mother's mirror. The flood
in our valley was not punishment; it meant

nothing. How it kissed our doorstep
and moved on meant nothing. I have no god

but this—the year of downpour, the way he wants
to become me, an orange ember I'll swallow

for its glow. Moon so free of a human
face, I will be unable to look away.

Droplet

He tells me if I were to watch someone
being pulled into a black hole
all I would see was them forever falling,
hardly moving. A girl
suspended in neither liquid nor air.
She is careening and static. She does not age
at all. I want him
to be more than himself.

That night, my dreams make loose
loops of time. A battered Ford pickup, a white
German shepherd barking hoarse on the end
of a chain, a field of tall grass my sisters and I
run through, our legs latticed
with scratches. My father leaves me
a series of messages asking me to come to a show
he's playing in Tennessee until he realizes
he's in a cancer ward until he realizes he's already
dead until I realize he never called at all.

In the morning, I see a spider by a drop
of water on the bathroom floor.
When I realized she's drinking
from it, it's enough to stop me
from killing her.

Lion's Mane

In the water off the cliffs of Rosario Head,
I spot a jellyfish. Brick red and apricot

orange, its edges undefined. They come
to this sheltered bay at the end of summer

to die. Each year when fall returns, I dream
of the labyrinthine. The past and future

distended and turned inside out, grinning
bone and gristle exposed. Hairlike strands hang

from the bell of the jellyfish. No blood,
no brain, no nervous system. Though I miss you

more than my mouth can hold at once
to say, I don't think we're made for anything

in particular, meant for anyone in particular.
The jellyfish moves like an atomic cloud.

Nebulous, lovely, indifferent. Who I loved before you,
who I'll love after—they all dissolve and I drink

and drink of them. Later, I read that the Lion's
Mane jellyfish can grow tentacles longer

than a blue whale. I read about how they
trap their prey by spreading these strands

so wide. How they have eight rhopalia, organs
to help them balance. How they glow at night.

C, there is so much I still want
to tell you about, including this creature

                            that can produce its own light.

In retrospect, I dream of our wedding

called off. Then the valley fills
with water and your mother's

gloating teeth. Black spiders the size
of my face follow me like dogs as I set out.

Now, I wonder: What was so wrong
with redemption? The light

-flooded room, we could live there
despite the salt and copper levels

in our brains. Injured or healing, two
sides of a coin that never lands. What did I lose

in our game? The number of bones
that make up a hand. The broken glass I hid

beneath my dress. Almost every memory
of you laughing. The way rain ran

down the windshield of your truck and I didn't
even try to explain constellation. *You can't control*

anything, I'd tell you now, years
gone still, anger just an imprint in my skull,

the reasons all dried up, *but how you explain
your loss of control.*

When you first ask if we can have a child

I've seen you undress in the yard, watched rain
turn to steam and rise off your skin. I've learned not to tell you

too often how overwhelmed I am by my want
for you. While the dog sleeps, her tail knocks against the floor
and I think about how we cannot always have access
to the happiness of those we love.

If we have a child, who will raise her? Certainly not the ghost
of a father I hardly spoke to. Certainly not the wolves you
    swear
you see circling me when you happen to wake in the night.

Think of where I came from—think
of the anger I've only recently set down beside a river
seething with silt. There are rooms for this kind of grief.

Some people fill whole houses with it.

*

I leave strips of paper and fistfuls of hair from my brush
for the flock of Steller's Jays in our yard
but they won't take these offerings. They want me to resist
the impulse to intervene.

In the car one night—constellations turning, country road
turning—I say, *If we have a child,*
you will love it more than me.

You don't deny it. The ringing of bells passes through
the body and comes out as the sobs of a mother
behind a closed door. But what if nothing

is possession? Could I imagine a way out of myself then?

*

When I spot the wasp nest under the eaves
of our cabin, I wait for the sun to set
and then spray it with poison. I watch how the nest foams,
watch the wasps drop to the earth
one by one. Later, I cannot articulate my guilt to you

but I try. If we have a child, who will raise her? These trees
surround us on three sides. The river takes the fourth.

Tell me you believe our bodies together make a jar
that can hold light. Tell me you believe in love without leaving.
Winter without an underside of bruises.

The first snow of autumn falls and my heart crosses
the river in the black mouth of a crow. Praise the sorrow
-clogged throat. Praise this chain of howls
that rips across the mountainside.

I reach in the churning belly
of the oil drum stove and pull out the baby
you've been dreaming of.

A rewriting of our last goodbye

In one version of this story, I have a spine.
I try to keep it
straight as the wall swallows
the door you leave through.

After, I wander the alleys
and archways of my mind trying
to coax years I lost back
into the rabbit hole of my mouth.

In another version, you kiss
my dog's head, tell her,
I'll be seeing you.
In one version, this is
the last time I ever see you.

Or, you bury the boar's head
that grew between us while we slept.

In the morning, I dig it up, grow intimate
with the rot.

In another, I finally say, *I'm sorry.*
From the bedroom, a round, beveled mirror
overhears me and laughs.

In another, we have
a son. Or, you have a son
with someone else. When I touch
him, his skin burns my hand.
When I touch him, he screams
and blossoms into a man
who carries his anger like a pickaxe
over the shoulder.

With it, he'll till a garden, mine
a mountain, join a dead man's war.

Or, you are my family.
Or, love is dry riverbed
that we keep returning to,
our bodies twisted with thirst.

In one version of this story, I live
by an ocean where the tide
brings news of the world. I am not
any man's siren.

I put my hand in the water, reach
for the blades of bull kelp. There are forests
of it here, whole labyrinths

beneath the surface. In this one,
I finally show myself
some mercy.

Bald Eagle on Blue Stones

When I find him, he's eating. Feasting, really. White feathers of what I believe to be an eviscerated mew gull all around him. It is dawn. The nation trawls its sicknesses; everything as we know it has to end. I'm tired of living

in my head. I saddle a driftwood log—dry, sun-scoured—and inch closer to the eagle still halfway down the beach. A man I loved finally sends an apology like a paper boat across the sea. And here I am, still pouring my anger down a drain one teaspoon at a time.

I've seen him before, this eagle, spiraling over urchin rocks. Oystercatchers, cormorants, and bufflehead ducks eying him uneasily. King of all these stones. Perhaps you were never as sick as you thought. Perhaps, I was never as cruel.

The eagle sees me but won't leave his gutted prey, his prize. Imagine, the soft throat of nothing. Imagine I'm still gunning for you.

When I lie in bed at night, the low roar of the water never stops. This dreaming never stops.

After the horses are gone

Your face is more mask than dreamer. There is no girl
to feel inside your mouth, count your teeth.

You sleep heavy and thoughtless as the stones you gave me
when you wanted to know earth's substance and structure.

After the horses are gone, your mother calls
but you don't answer. You call your father but he doesn't answer.

You shiver like a warbler caught in the rafters
of an abandoned copper mine during a storm. Wolves

still ask for each other but we do not
stand between their voices. Everything we individually witness

has no witness. After the horses are gone, there's no one
to blame. I stuff my mouth with glass. Use it to kiss anyone

who'll have me. They twitch and talk in their sleep. I save
all of it in my mother's jars. After the horses are gone, you

write out *isolation* in loopy cursive like a lover's name.
I lift my talking head from my neck, wedge it

between branches. Juncos move
like mice in the end-of-season snow.

A Litany of Dreams You May Borrow

The one where I pick sunlight off my skin like scales or sequins

Or I have a boy's torso and a jaw
        that doesn't lock when I start to laugh

Any of the dreams with snakes or my mother
trapped in a radiator vent
        because they spring from the same well

My little sister and I are teenagers again, still speaking
to each other, and she climbs a sugar
maple and never comes back

The ones where rain comes through the roof
but not the ones where it is snowing in my room

S and I still live together but a gray horse
circles the house, starving
        No one names it

My father is in a hospice bed, holding up
his rot-dappled organs one by one
        as offerings to me

The cow pasture
       where I'm in a wedding dress
       carrying a pitcher of his blood

B and I are back on the beach at night
and she kisses me except this time ocean
is made of milk and sweet

No one invents sin so we sun ourselves on the rooftop

Any dream of my grandfather—that skull
for a face, the parrot watching on, the white
sheet and long fingernails
       In fact, you may keep them, convince yourself
       there is a lesson

The dream where the brakes gave out
The dream where the brakes gave out

His head is in my lap and the window
is open even though it is January outside

A war between nations of men takes place
in my mother's dining room
       My sisters and I watch from beneath a table

Those you can leave: any dream where he says my name
        aloud or his mouth is against my hair, any dream
        where the dead forgive

The first girl I loved asking, *Are you sure*
you don't know me? until she disappears

The whole room slants and I fall from the bed
to the wall as if the house is trying to shake
me from itself like a parasite

The dream I had after S found the knife
I hid beneath the nightstand

The one where I saw our sons using sticks
as swords, their mouths yellow
        and I chose not to have them

The first gentle boy from my childhood is back and we are in love

When the church burns down and my sisters and I are blamed

The one where what I love is not unwell,
not in need at all, so I shrink to the size
of a kitchen ant and crawl away

Or, because of this, I am finally able to stay

My mother is my daughter and when she speaks, hummingbirds fill her mouth

The one where I actually forgive him and he leans back, finally rests his eyes, and says

There is no ending

Acknowledgments

I want to thank my family, especially my mother. Thank you to my communities in Bellingham and Marblemount, Washington. Thank you to my teachers and students at Hugo House.

Special thank you to Heather Warren, Freesia McKee, Alysia Li Ying Sawchyn, Crystal Ignatowski, Jithu Ramesh, Kendell Newman Sadiik, Piera Siegmann, Amy Casey, Megan Perra, Elle Gasperini, Sophia Kast, Becky Mandelbaum, Evan Holmstrom, and Calvin Laatsch.

Thank you to Blair and Lillet Press! My deepest gratitude to Ada Limón, Kelli Russell Agodon, and Denise Duhamel.

I am extremely grateful to the following publications where versions of these poems first appeared:

"Wellspring," *Newfound*

"Your Grandfather Killed a Deer, My Grandfather Killed a Deer," *Adroit*

"Buttercream," *Best of the Net 2020* and *The Hunger Journal*

"Daughter Knot," *Hoxie Gorge Review*

"On his deathbed, my father, who I haven't seen in ten years, offers me homemade moonshine" and "Song Dogs," *Anti-Heroin Chic*

"I know we're all sick of poems with deer but let me explain" and "A Litany of Dreams You May Borrow," *Yes, Poetry*

"Some thoughts on the one who said I expected too much," *decomP magazinE*

"Oxbow," *Split Rock Review*

"Leveret at Laughing Jaw" and "In which I dream I am my grandfather," *The Hunger Journal*

"Ember," *Fugue*

"Unvigil," *Red Wheelbarrow*

"Calf," "During the Wildfires," and "When you first ask if we can have a child," *The Fourth River: Tributaries, The New Nature*

"The houses where they eat the lambs," *Oxidant | Engine*

"A Poem to Multiple Men," *The Thought Erotic*

"Deer Season," *Talking Writing*

CPSIA information can be obtained
at www.ICGtesting.com
Printed in the USA
JSHW031518210122
22074JS00004B/5

9 781949 467789